D1572826

AMERICAN WINGSHOOTING

AMERICAN WINGSHOOTING

A TWENTIETH CENTURY PICTORIAL SAGA

Text and photography by

Ben O. Williams

Commentary by Charley F. Waterman

WILLOW CREEK PRESS

MINOCQUA, WISCONSIN

© 1998 Ben O. Williams
All rights reserved. No part of this book may be
reproduced or transmitted in any form by any
means, electronic or mechanical, including photo-
copying, recording, or by any information storage
and retrieval system, without permission in writing
from the Publisher.

Published by Willow Creek Press
P.O. Box 147, Minocqua, Wisconsin 54548

For information on other Willow Creek titles,
call 1-800-850-9453

Designed by Patricia Bickner Linder

Library of Congress Cataloging-in-Publication Data

Williams, Ben O.
    American wingshooting : a pictorial saga / by Ben O.
        Williams ; introduction by Charles F. Waterman.
        p.   cm.
    ISBN 1-57223-190-4
    1. Upland game bird shooting--United States. I. Title.
    SK323.W524   1998
    799.2'46'0973--dc21   98-39529
                                                      CIP

Printed in Canada

CONTENTS

ACKNOWLEDGMENTS

These people all living in different locations of the United States have gracefully shared their hunting haunts with me: Leigh Perkins, John Hughes, Wendell Holeman, Steve and Chris Smith, Drummond and Seth Hadley, Ben Brown, Dale and Lila Critz, Mark Kayser, Bill Vodenhal, Steve Nelson, John F. Nash, Mac Minnard, Jim Woolington, and Ken Marsh. Thanks to Steve Claiborn, Dave Meisner, Charley Waterman, Chris Hyle, Tom Petrie and many others for being hunting partners and photo models on my home turf. Also a special thanks to all the fine bird dogs that helped made this book possible.

DEDICATION

This book is dedicated to Williams' Pride Winston, who
pointed and retrieved every species of upland game bird
in North America. He was not only my best friend but
the best hunting companion I ever had.

FOREWORD

There was a half of box of faded red cardboard 12 gauge shotgun shells, number seven and half on the closet shelf in our vestibule that belonged to my grandfather. I was sure he would be back the following year to use the rest of the shotshells and maybe take me hunting again for pheasant and bobwhites along the railroad tracks in back of my home in northern Illinois. Periodically, I would pull a chair over to the closet, climb up on the seat, reach for the box and count the twelve shotshells left over from last years hunting. IÕd think about the good times I had tagging along with him hunting upland gamebirds and the stories he told about his English pointers. The year was 1939 and I was seven years old.

Ever since then I have been involved in some way with upland game birds. be it, training pointing dogs, hunting the different species or photographing and studying their habits and habitat.. That adds up to sixty years, or over half of this century in the fields, prairies, foothills, forest and mountains, of North America.

My love of bird dogs and the outdoors are the principal elements in my passion for hunting upland birds. To walk behind pointing dogs afield during the off season is as enjoyable as it is during the hunting season.

And the pleasure I take in the dogs finding and pointing the birds is as exciting as the shooting.

The nature of the game birds' habits, habitat, and the scenery that each species takes me into is first and foremost. The skill of the dogs and the relation of man and dog enjoying the hunt together is secondary, but also highly important.

After hunting game birds for more than a half century, I still remain a little squeamish about killing them. Clean kills are important to me; bag limits are not. Yet game birds must occasionally be killed, maybe to reward a dog, maybe to please the palate, or sometimes just to gratify man's need to hunt. But it is only a small part of the whole experience.

This book features hunting the different species of upland game birds in their natural habitat across North America. It is written and photographed with the hunter in mind who appreciates this wonderful field sport. No one book can cover all of the coverts, covers, prairies, deserts, wetlands, woodlands, farms, and ranches in which the upland game birds live.

I especially hope one of the essays calls to mind a place you hunted, be it with a friend, son, daughter, or maybe a hunting story once told by your father or grandfather.

— Ben O. Williams, 1998

The Twentieth Century

Upland bird hunting is an American tradition handed down from generation to generation. The highest pleasures of nature comes not from the killing but from an appreciation of all living and nonliving things around us.

Say "hunting," and most visualize big game hunting. Say "bird hunting," and it becomes colloquial — pheasant in the bottom lands, sage grouse in mule deer country, bobwhite quail on the Atlantic shores, ruffed grouse in the hardwoods, Huns in the vast, rolling wheat fields, ptarmigan in the snow fields, and western quail in the desert.

More than twenty gallinaceous species come under the category of "game birds." Sportsmen call them "upland game birds," which means legal game that may be taken during an open hunting season. Nearly all of the gallinaceous birds in North America fall into one large group, the pheasant family (*Phasianidae*), which includes grouse, pheasants, quail, partridge, and turkey. The pigeon family, (*Columbidae*), and woodcock, of the sandpiper family (*Scolopacidae*), are also game birds of the uplands. Native gallinaceous birds were once distributed throughout North America and one or more species occupied almost every type of natural

ecosystem in the country. Just as man produced many different varieties of chickens, most from a single species, nature produced many different species of wild game birds. Natural selection (breeding) was controlled by the environment, and only the birds that adapted to their surroundings survived to breed more of their kind. Usually an individual species of game bird is restricted to a geographical region, such as woodlands, prairie, desert, or tundra. In most instances, once the bird is locked into its environment through selective breeding, it will not survive when moved to an altogether different ecosystem, even if a similar subspecies once lived there.

Two exceptions are the native bobwhite quail and prairie chicken, which took advantage of changing environments by following the plow. The bobwhite, truly a bird of the small farm and a gleaner of grain, broadened its range south and southwestward on the heels of the sodbusters, while the greater prairie chicken, a bird of the open country, gradually extended its

range westward along with the homesteaders. Even though new types of habitat created by man became occupied by some native species, many others could not adapt, and therefore became extinct.

The prairie chicken has been more associated with the open plains rather than with open parks of the woodlands. Those familiar with the rolling prairie of days gone by will never forget the love-making antics of the male each spring, their low booming sound carrying for miles across the tall-grass prairies at daybreak.

Only a century ago, North America had a greater number and variety of game birds than any country in the world. Even though the records of men killing more than a hundred woodcock in a single day and shooting a wagon load of prairie chickens not far from New York City seems impossible today, it happened and on

a grand scale. Consider that Massachusetts once had a bounty on ruffed grouse because the bird was thought to be harmful to fruit crops. Kentucky regarded prairie grouse as a pest. During this period, — called The Golden Age of Bird Hunting — bag and possession limits were nonexistent, and the hunting season was open year- round. Shooting occurred day after day, and the number of birds bagged was staggering.

By 1900, large-scale market hunting was drawing to a close. Even though game birds could still be sold, a federal law passed in 1918 put an end to the selling of wild birds. Two years later, the measure withstood various court tests, and the market hunter turned to other ways of making a living. Still, few states had any bag or possession limits, and seasons never closed.

By the turn of the century, the human population of the United States had doubled, and many people moved to the outlying areas and put more land under the plow, built more roads, cleared more woodlands, and drained marshes. As a result of these vast changes in the landscape, some creatures fared better than others. But wildlife habitat diminished.

When the great populations of the ruffed grouse, wild turkey, quail, and heath hen plummeted on the East Coast, hunting seasons and regulations were enacted to stop the decline. Regulations shortened seasons and shooting hours, reduced bag limits, and prohibited the use of bird dogs for hunting. Most people believed that once hunting seasons and regulation were implemented and predators controlled, the birds would return in their former numbers. Unfortunately the loss of habitat was never a consideration, so the problem continued.

The extinction of the passenger pigeon occurred in the early 1900s, due to the bird's loss of habitat, not from hunting pressure. They had once been widespread throughout the East. With the cutting of the hardwood forests and clearing the land for farming, the bird's habitat — their roosting and nesting grounds — shrank. This magnificent bird could not adapt to its new surroundings, and, consequently, the last known passenger pigeon died in 1914.

The heath hen, once a prolific subspecies of the greater prairie chicken, experienced much the same fate. With the rapid growth of civilization, this fine New England game bird retreated to its last suitable habitat on Martha's Vineyard, an island off the coast of Massachusetts. Several years later, the last heath hen died without fanfare.

With the arrival of more people in the Midwest, more land went under the plow and much of the tall-grass prairie vanished. Prairie grouse, once an important food source for homesteaders, could be easily obtained. But by the early 1900s, most of the pinnate grouse booming grounds and the sharp-tailed grouse dancing grounds were silent.

The westward expansion by settlers followed the cattle barons. By the turn of the century, grazing was widespread in the West, with large livestock companies running herds on the range year-round. The vast herds of bison were already gone, marking one of the most tragic losses of a natural resource in history. During the last years of the buffalo slaughter, public reaction to uncontrolled hunting fostered a movement for a wildlife conservation program. This movement resulted in hunting laws in the West on not only big game but also on game birds. But for the most part, the new laws enacted by Congress were ignored by most settlers or not enforced. Though many of these laws were largely ignored, they mark the birthplace of wildlife conservation.

Farming and ranching increased in the West on land once used only by wildlife. Much of this land was public, unwanted by the settlers and only used for the grazing of cattle. During this period, managers of public land did little for game bird habitat or management. The serious drought of the 1930s, poor farming practices, and widespread overgrazing by livestock during these years contributed to the loss of valuable habitat. Few people associated land use practices with loss of wildlife habitat, and therefore habitat was destroyed at a alarming rate. The decline of upland game birds in many areas of the West followed the same pattern as the game birds of the East.

When native upland game bird populations declined across the country, restocking attempts of some native species where first made in the East, then in the West. Most were failures. Sportsmen and landowners started looking for substitute species as replacements. Many exotic game birds, such as European quail, peacock, and guinea fowl were planted by private individuals, conservation clubs, and state fish and game departments. These efforts largely failed in North America's unforgiving and harsh environment.

Just prior to 1900, the successful stocking of pheasants in Oregon encouraged other states and hunting clubs throughout the nation to stock this beautiful game bird. It is impossible to estimate the number of non-native game birds stocked throughout the country. After hundreds of attempts, the pheasant and the Hungarian partridge were established in several locations in which the habitat was similar to the bird's native land. Once established, the birds' offspring spread to surrounding areas of suitable habitat.

Inevitably, the percentage of successful stocking was so low and so costly that most such efforts were discontinued. Primarily because of a newly unified outcry of sportsmen, many state game departments created upland game bird hatcheries and rearing facilities, and released thousands of mature pheasants each year just before the hunting seasons. This put-and-take pheasant hunting was expensive, but it did fill a

void for the sportsmen for many years. However, it did nothing to establish wild populations.

Years ago it was recognized that stocking pen-raised game birds did not work. Efforts to establish new populations with wild-trapped game birds did succeed. But little was known about how to catch them. In the early years, live-trapping was crude, so the number of captured birds was always low. But after years of trial and error, more sophisticated live-trapping methods were developed. Suddenly, wild birds were not so hard to catch and stocking them become so successful that it helped to reestablish native game birds to some of their original range.

Capturing wild game birds was so cost-efficient compared to raising game birds in rearing facilities it was used in marginal habitat. Consider for a moment the wild turkey. Through live-trapping, restocking all of the five native subspecies of wild turkey throughout its original range was possible, as well as was establishing ranges where turkeys never lived before. Today, all but a few states have a wild turkey population and wild turkey hunting, thanks to biological research programs and to organizations such as The Wild Turkey Federation.

In the early years of wild game bird restoration, state game agencies relied on recommendations from local sportsmen and other members of a community within a district. Most recommendations had no basis in sound conservation and many were politically motivated. Local game wardens were the conservation officers yet were untrained in scientific game management. Little was known about ecology, and the biological needs of wildlife were overlooked because a management program based on biology was not available.

A few conservationists with biology backgrounds realized that the elimination of predators had little effect on the game populations. It was theorized that an ecological understanding of habitat and wildlife management was not such a simple problem. Rudimentary studies showed that game populations decrease or increase according to the amount of habitat available, regardless of predators or human hunting pressure. But for years, most studies fell on deaf ears.

The conservation practices of the day were limited primarily to predator control, releasing pen-raised birds, and law enforcement. People begin realizing that something more had to be done to save our precious wildlife. However, most states had neither the power nor the money to meet this need.

Public outcry in 1937 caused Congress to pass the Federal Aid in Wildlife Restoration (Pittman-Robertson) Act. This earmarked funds from a special excise tax on sporting arms and ammunition for wildlife management by the states. For the first time, funds were available to hire trained game biologists to address the real problems affecting wildlife. Studies were initiated to determine the relationships between game and its environment and how to best manage the wildlife.

These game management programs had a slow start, but over the years they have done more for wildlife and increased game populations than any other factor in this century.

The growth in human population has had a large effect on the loss of habitat. Once, more people lived and worked in rural areas than in cities. These population shifts from rural areas to towns sometimes helped wildlife. The countryside was once dotted with red barns and rural

schools. Small family farms with many out-buildings, wind breaks, and fields intersected by dirt lanes or fencerows were once part of the rural American scene. One hundred acres was all one man could work; a one- or two-bottom plow could till only so much earth in a day. So fields were small, crops were diversified, and the wide edges surrounding the crops were good wildlife habitat. As the decades passed, both farms and fields became larger, with fewer fencerows and less natural habitat. Family farms gave way to agribusiness, which plowed miles of country and planted single crops. Farm machinery kept pace in size, with their huge rubber tires and giant thirty- foot chisel plows. So called "clean farming" was born.

As agribusiness also moved west to the prairie states, big tractors tilled hundreds of acres of sagebrush, turning it into dryland farms. Such operations depend on endless fallow strips of land that lay idle to collect precious moisture for next year's crop. These environmental disasters leave no vegetation edges for wildlife of any kind.

Again, hunting and predation has little effect on the decline or increase of game bird populations. But conditions such as drought, radical seasonal weather changes, and habitat loss have had a profound effect on wildlife populations. If the prairie grouse and partridge were to fade away — and they're still losing ground — the birds would undoubtedly be missed by many. On the other hand — as demonstrated by the extinction of the passenger pigeon and the heath hen — the bereavement

would probably be short-lived. In this age of rapidly increasing human population, most people have little concern for the prairie game bird's welfare. Fortunately, there are still some prairie grasslands that have sparse human populations, which is important for the birds' survival. Most of these are federal and state lands, and these may well be the last stronghold of our native game birds.

This great continent of North America is certainly big, but drive along the back roads of the West and look closely: the country may be large but wildlife habitat is shrinking at a alarming rate. For every sidewalk, paved road, parking lot, or hiking trail, we have lost a little more of nature's natural cover for wildlife.

The first part of this century was disastrous for upland game birds. The latter part has shown some evidence of repair. Taking land out of production and resting or returning it to its natural state of prairie grasslands, woodlands, riparian waterways, and wetlands has helped wildlife tremendously. Federal programs designed to do just that, such as the Soil Bank Program of the past and today's CRP (Conservation Reserve Program) have helped wildlife.

In the latter part of the 20th century, new methods and programs have been implemented with good results. The emphasis has been in the right direction of reestablishing habitat or minimizing its loss. Controlled burning, fencing out cattle from riparian areas, planting trees and food plots, and resting or rotating lands from grazing and planting all have helped the return of upland game birds to some of their original

range. State game departments have purchased or compensated landowners with money from hunting licenses to help improve game bird habitat. Managers of our public lands (BLM, Forest Service, and state owned) now employ wildlife biologists and implement conservation programs to manage wildlife habitat on these lands. New concepts that benefit wildlife are being used in many areas. But even though progress has been made for multiple use on our public lands, we have a long way to go.

State and federal agencies and private industry are providing more support for research. Many individuals have joined groups that recognized the wake-up call to save wildlife and habitat before it's to late. Organizations such

as the Ruffed Grouse Society, Ducks Unlimited, Pheasants Forever, Quail Unlimited and even local hunting and bird dog clubs have all had a great impact on the recovery of our game bird habitat. Outdoor sporting goods and arms manufacturers, sporting goods stores, sporting magazines, hunting book publishers, and newspapers also have become aware of the importance of improving habitat for wildlife.

The popularity of upland bird hunting is growing by leaps and bounds. Spending time hunting with your dog, a friend, or your children is still a great American tradition. I certainly hope the 21st century will be good bird hunting for our next generation. Man now controls the destiny of all of our wildlife.

Part One

Wetlands and
Woodlands

Wetlands and Woodlands

Introduction

by Charley F. Waterman

The bobwhite quail and the ruffed grouse are America's game bird royalty, with little in common as to habits or habitat.

Ruffed grouse gunners do not go in crowds. They are likely to be quiet people with secret coverts. Some of the bobwhite hunting is social, the shooting parties going forth from their plantation "big houses" with rubber-tired gunning wagons and stump-broke mules. The Southern bobwhite can be the nation's most expensive game bird. But the Northern grouse seeker and the bobwhite follower are often the same person with only minor changes in uniform. The same open-bored gun can serve for both birds.

And both birds belong with dogs, generally dogs that point, and some say it's setters for grouse and pointers for quail. But time and breeding have changed that, producing pointers that softwalk the old New England apple orchards, and setters that become flowing streaks across peanut patches. And then there are the "new" breeds that have brought their own traditions from Europe or elsewhere.

Ruffed grouse are known as "cycle" birds, but their welfare has also been dependent upon farming and timber practices and human population changes. In general, their distribution has not changed greatly, although there are fewer birds than there once were. But the Southeastern quail's habitat patterns are new because of clean farming, hunting pressure, and unknowns that puzzle game managers.

Where wild quail have become scarce, the private game preserve has imitated the aristocrat's plantation, generally using pen-raised birds that

have been developed to closely imitate wild ones. But there is a loser in that process. In most of the South the gunner who hunted after work no longer has a place to shoot and few family pointers trot along the farm-town streets today.

Reproduction of pen-raised quail is very sketchy in the wild, and some biologists believe that the "tame" birds carry genes that degrade wild coveys. In some cases they point to visibly inferior internal organs in quail that may be many generations removed from wild bob-whites. While the private plantations provide wild birds at great expense and the public or semi-public preserves continually improve the quality of their game, the brushpatcher and his beloved and scarred "meat dog" find they must lease land or leave the sport. The status and

geography of bobwhite hunting has changed dramatically for better or worse.

When Herbert L. Stoddard wrote a thorough text on the bobwhite in 1941, the Midwest was considered a secondary residence for the bird and Texas was listed as marginal habitat. Even when Walter Rosene's somewhat similar volume appeared in 1969, Texas was considered worthwhile only in the better years. It is true that Texas is a boom-and-bust bobwhite state, dependent upon weather. But in the best years the wild quail shooting there is incredibly good. In Texas' brush country it is easy to look over a pointing dog and imagine the ghost of a 19th century cowboy chasing a longhorn steer, and there is likely to be a covey where a crumbling ranch house is marked by its windmill's skeleton. The Midwest has come on as well, and it may be that the Southeast is being replaced as bobwhite mecca.

A little-known upland quail is the Mearn's, also known as Montezuma or Harlequin, of the Southwest (There are other names and similar birds both north and south of the border). It is the tightest holder of all, living on oak ridges high above the desert country for the most part and, with neat excavations, feeding on choice tubers. The Mearn's holds so tightly a pointing dog may appear to be on a mouse hunt.

The ruffed grouse hunter is generally a woodcock hunter as well, the ruff often leaving with thunder while the woodcock, really a relative of shorebirds, can seem to pedal his way through the alder tops with an eerie wing whisper. Although the ruff is generally a resident and the "timberdoodle" a furtive migrator, they appear together in most localities. So sacred is the game that some woodcock lovers feel that "timberdoodle" is an insulting name.

The woodcock's migration is almost an ethereal event that depends on temperature and winds, and there are great concentrations of birds where a frustrated dog seems mesmerized by ghostly wing sounds. The next morning there may be only worming holes and chalk marks. But these movements are noted and recorded by the faithful gunners, and the master will announce that the young aspen need one more year or that the trees are "too old" and he knows of a place a few miles away where the more recent cutover will be just right.

In more ways than one, the grouse, bobwhite, and woodcock gunners are much the same, although they may have some conflicting opinions. The guns are light and quick, and at least one authority wrote that only a 20 gauge double gun was sportsmanlike for quail. His ballistic knowledge was skimpy, for typical 20-gauge charges can be had in 12, 16, and 28 gauge. The 20 gauge side-by-side is traditional for private quail plantations, but there are honorably scarred lightweights of other silhouettes in grouse camps and plantation gun racks.

A View from the Wagon

Judging from the sportsman's point of view of yesteryear, the bobwhite was once at the head of the list, and for good reason. Few other game birds meet all of the hunter and pointing dog requirements. Even today the bobwhite is still the king of the species. Quail are covey birds and seldom venture far from where they were born. The bird lies well for pointing dogs and flushes with a fury of feathers. Small and fast in flight, it offers a difficult target. Do you remember when your dog pointed a clump of grass, almost touching the golden carpet as you kicked the cover several times? Then, to your surprise, they flushed and your gun was not ready.

The bobwhite is a native of North America and was once widely distributed. The bobwhite became plentiful when the land was cultivated and open areas intermixed with the hardwood forest.

According to early accounts, settlers along the Atlantic Coast used the bird as a food supply. When the pioneers moved to the Northwest Territory and conquered much of the forest, the grain belt broadened and the quail followed. They are truly a bird of the small farm, a gleaner, ridding the crops of insects and content with the grain left on the ground during harvest.

Today most of the bobwhite hunting in the eastern United States takes place in the southern coastal states, on plantations managed exclusively for quail. Some have wild birds, some use pen-raised birds, but all are by fee or invitation. Much of the bird's habitat is heavy undergrowth in pine forests.

In the spring, the call of the male can be heard, but sightings are only occasional, maybe a glimpse of him on a fence post close to a tangle of briars. When the birds flush, they fly to the thickest cover. Southern pointing dogs work close and shooting is quick.

The habits and the habitat of the bobwhite in the Midwest differ from their Southeastern cousins, but it is still the same fine game bird. In the Midwest, where the crops and open prairie merge with riparian forest along waterways and brushy draws, the bobwhite is at home. Hedges and windbreaks of Osage orange, Russian olives, caragana, and green ash are some of his favorite hiding places on the prairie, close to where farmers store grains. Springtime in the prairie states is the time folks become acquainted with the bobwhite. He is a common sight on fence posts along rural roads that intersect the farms of the Midwest.

The prairie is open, pointing dogs run big, and shooting is under a gigantic blue sky. It's easy to underestimate the speed of a quail in open country heading for the nearest cover and disappearing before a shot is fired.

In the South, the air is crisp in January and the
big pines with their aromatic fragrance glisten in
the sunlight. When hunting plantation country
the day is spent with mules, bird dogs, guns, and
bobwhite quail. Nowhere is the hunt held in
higher regard.

*Once tallgrass and mixed prairie covered
the Midwest. Settlers moved westward and
the bobwhite quail followed the plow,
making it their home. Most stone houses,
built by men who tilled the soil, are gone,
but the bobwhite quail is still abundant.*

Grouse Amongst Fall Colors

he ruffed grouse has long been a resident of the northern and boreal forests of North America. They are the most widely distributed native game bird across a large part of the continent. The bird's range is vast, occurring naturally from Alabama to Labrador in the east and from California to Alaska in the west. This fine game bird occupies much of the Canadian provinces and more than thirty states. It lives in some of the most isolated country in North America, but it can also show up at your doorstep. Ruffed grouse are non-migratory and spend their entire short life within a small area.

Ruffed grouse are birds of forest succession, forests kept young by natural or man made ecological disasters.

Ruffed grouse country anywhere is special, but the Northeastern hardwood forest can hold the hunter spellbound, especially when the leaves turn a rainbow of flaming colors, highlighting the small rural farms, abandoned orchards deep in the woods, and overgrown fields circled with mossy stone walls built by homesteaders long ago. Logging the tall, mature woodlands opened the canopy for the growth of understory, and the grouse moved in. To the Great Lakes hunter, ruffed grouse cover means brilliant fall colors, slash clearings, alder stands, logging roads, paper birch, and crossbuck fences. To the Western ruffed grouse hunter, golden quakies outlined by evergreen forests, steep slopes, rocky outcropping, buck brush, crystal creeks, or cattle tails to ridge tops are familiar. The boreal forest is the home of the Canadian and Alaskan grouse hunter, who walks the lonely trails between the willow slaps that are mostly used by moose and bear, or works the edges of the forest clearings. But no matter where they hunt, ruffed grouse hunters are pretty much alike, with double guns and pointing dogs

The best grouse hunting weather for both man and dog is a bright, crisp autumn day after a hard frost. Ruffed grouse are not early risers, so there is no need to be out at the crack of dawn. He is for the gentle bird hunter, but only on his terms. For you are in the grouse's living room, and the bird knows all the escape routes well. If I were to choose the outcome between the hunter and the ruffed grouse, I would have to favor the grouse.

Most of the eastern forest of United States was cleared for farming and for logging. Today, much of the same forest has grown back to what it once was. Ruffed grouse hunters look for certain types of habitat, like old apple orchards or cut over cover within the dense forest. The grouse hunter knows that quick perception and accurate shooting is his key to a successful hunt.

Tamaracks and Timberdoodles

The woodcock belongs to a large family of shore birds and is the only shore bird that is considered an upland game bird. Unlike the rest of the species, woodcock have adapted to woodland habitat. Woodcock are migratory and live in the forested regions of eastern Canada and the eastern United States. Their range approximates the Atlantic and Mississippi migration routes of waterfowl. The bird summers in the north and winters in the south, but much of this range overlaps. This elusive bird passes through much of the eastern portions of ruffed grouse range on its migratory flight south. The bird's migratory patterns and staging areas make for some of the finest upland bird shooting in the East. When flushed, it rises vertically to clear the brush, levels off, and after a short flight gracefully flutters back to the ground. When approached, the bird depends on its camouflage coloration for concealment and holds tightly rather than flying.

The woodcock's habitat is mostly regrowth forest from burns, clearcuts, and woodlands cleared by homesteaders. The bird prefers areas of lowlands surrounded by shrubs and young forests. The main diet of the timberdoodle is earthworms, which it finds by probing moist soil with its long bill. The areas along streams, ponds, and seeps, thick patches of high brush with little ground vegetation, and damp ground is some of the timberdoodle's favorite places. When a big flight of woodcock is in progress on its way south, large numbers of birds will concentrate in the same feeding and resting areas year after year.

The experienced woodcock hunter is a master at finding the bird's cover because he knows the bird's food. A hunter who finds such a place usually keeps the spot a secret and checks the location the same time every season. A good timberdoodle hunter spends much time looking at the ground. Woodcock leave many telltale signs. Fresh bore holes tell you they're near. Watch for other signs such as tracks, droppings, and dusting places.

Pointers and setters are traditional for hunting woodcock because the bird sets well. The camouflage color and the heavy cover makes it very difficult to locate a downed bird. A retriever is essential. When you knock down a woodcock, give the dog a chance to find the bird without laying down your own scent. Woodcock may not be fast flyers, but the colloquial name, timberdoodle, fits the woodcock well. Its erratic flight pattern through underbrush can lower any shooter's score.

After the first frost, tamaracks change color from green to bright gold. By then the alders have dropped their leaves and the first wave of woodcock have come out of the north. This is the time the woodcock hunter walks the woods, following the dog closely, for the dog knows the hiding places of woodcock better than the hunter.

Quail of the Evergreen Oaks

The oddest looking North American quail is the Mearn's, with its clown-like plumage. The Mearn's quail was once called the harlequin or clown quail because the bird's coloration resembles a comic performer in a pantomime who wears multi-colored, spangled garments. The call of the Mearn's is also like a comic performer, with a ventriloquist quality that makes it extremely difficult to pinpoint the bird's location.

In Mexico it's named after the last Aztec emperor, Montezuma, and rightly so, for this is a majestically handsome bird. No other quail is like it in appearance. The male has bold white and black stripes on the sides of the face, with white and black polka dots down the breast and sides.

As a game bird in the United States, it is not well known, primarily because of its solitary life style, its limited range, and its habit of lying still when approached. A native, the Mearn's northern range is southern Arizona, Texas, and New Mexico. The largest portion of the bird's range is in Old Mexico.

The home range of the Mearn's quail is as beautiful as the bird. The quail lives in grassy oak-pine canyons, on wooded mountain slopes, and in rocky ravines with dense underbrush. It is seldom found below 4,000 feet and is often found as high as 9,000 feet.

Like the bobwhite, it is a bird for pointers and setters. In good cover, a whole covey of Mearn's quail will sit tight for a pointing dog and the bird can often be approached to within a foot before flushing. The Mexicans sometimes call them little bobwhite because they sit so tight.

In my experience hunting Mearn's quail, the coveys lie better for a pointing dog than any other North American game bird. When a covey does flush, the birds usually

scatter. Singles will sit so tight that a hunter can pass within inches and not flush or see them. A dog with a keen nose that likes to work singles is ideal, and the same goes for locating downed birds. They're fast flyers and can twist and turn though an oak woods with ease. The bird is a wonderful target and can leave a shooter scratching his head.

All North American quail are beautiful and great to hunt, but as a game bird the Mearn's quail may be the most challenging. It's certainly a trophy quail. Hunting them is close to the top of my list of game birds, not for the killing, but for taking me places the Aztecs traveled.

Double guns, light loads, pointing dogs and Mearn's quail go together. I believe the Mearn's quail is an offspring of the wind that whispers in the evergreen oaks and turns the lonely windmills.

Wings of Fall

The mourning dove is a grand upland game bird. A member of the pigeon family, it is the only game bird that lives in all of the lower forty-eight states and six Canadian provinces.

Settlers encountered the bird wherever they went, but it was of little use to them for food. It is not a bird of the open prairie or the deep forest, but a resident of the riparian woodlands and the edges of the forest.

Doves are migratory and most of the northern birds winter in the southern states. Late summer, small flocks assemble in the north country and start their migration southward, joining together to form large groups. Many birds have already moved south before the fall dove hunting season opens in the northern states.

In their northern range, dove hunting has never had as much recognition as hunting the ruffed grouse or pheasant. Dove shooting is a pastime, mostly done by a lone hunter dressed in camo, concealed behind an old wooden fence, a hay bale, or a windmill. Most shooting takes place in a grain field or from a makeshift blind at the edge of a watering hole.

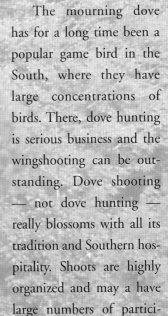

The mourning dove has for a long time been a popular game bird in the South, where they have large concentrations of birds. There, dove hunting is serious business and the wingshooting can be outstanding. Dove shooting — not dove hunting — really blossoms with all its tradition and Southern hospitality. Shoots are highly organized and may a have large numbers of participants, depending on the size of the dove field. Some fields accommodate several hundred people. Doves are highly gregarious and use only one feeding field at a time.

Shoots are formal and are announced weeks in advance. On the day of the outing, the guests gather, usually around noon, for an afternoon hunt. After blinds, stands, and stations are drawn or assigned, the hunters are taken to their locations. Gunners are placed around the field to keep the birds moving. Once the field has been shot, it is rested for several days so the birds can return for the next shoot.

The mourning dove is a swift, strong flier whose whistling sound in flight distinguishes it from all other game birds. It has an erratic fight pattern, making it one of the most challenging game birds for the gunner. A dove can change direction with a flap of its wing. I don't believe there is any other game bird that requires a faster swing of the gun. Good dove shooters are few. Doves are small and easily lost when downed. The hunting dog is a Southern tradition and dove shooting and dogs go together.

There are two kinds of upland game bird hunting: walk up hunting and stationary hunting. Dove hunting in the south is stationary, but also the most difficult shooting. This field sport is a highly organized southern tradition.

Part Two
Grasslands, Foothills, and Farmlands

Grasslands, Foothills, and Farmlands

Introduction

by Charley F. Waterman

America's most popular upland bird is an Oriental, the Chinese pheasant, outshining native game birds with his raucous voice and gaudy plumage, and it is gunned with rusty pump guns and inlaid custom double guns. Shooters may wear patched coveralls or British tweed. The American birds may be driven by paid beaters in imitation of European nobility. They may also be stalked by pointing dogs on brushy mountainsides, or they may be handled by near-military formations in cornfields.

Ringnecks can be raised like domestic chickens or they can be chased through frosty sloughs, but they have been a biologist's nightmare,

choosing certain home ranges with enthusiasm and refusing others that appear the same. There are wondrous pheasant dogs of many sizes and of unknown ancestry, and there are costly and well-trained thoroughbreds that have been reduced to helpless neurotics by only a few hours of pheasant contact. The question of whether pointers or flushers are better for pheasants is not settled after more than a century of debate.

In the prairie and sage country, most of the game birds were there when the wagons went west; most of them were simply called "chickens." It was on the grasslands where commercial gunners followed enormous flights of prairie grouse that moved ahead like rolling feathered waves. The true prairie chicken barely survived

the western surge that broke the sod that had formed its home. The sharp-tailed grouse fared better, adapting well to the winding draws with brush and trees that border cultivated land and seam the cow country. Game management has saved the prairie chicken from extermination.

The two birds are often hunted together and mixed coveys are common. With chickens not noted for close holding, pointing dogs are important, and it is no place for dainty guns and loads. There are times when serious operators manage to learn daily feeding routes and do their shooting without much walking — and pointing dogs aren't necessary. For the shooter who has studied the prairie birds, it is difficult to watch a restless airborne flock without imagining buffalo in the background, and he may imagine his own wagon creaking behind him.

Sharptails and true prairie chickens are addicted to short migrations and there are times when it is almost impossible to approach within range. Then there are times when singles and small coveys hold like bobwhite quail — or even tighter.

Fitting his land of sky and sage, the sage grouse seems a leftover from another era. The largest cocks may weigh seven pounds, and the sage hen's country is big. There are likely to be antelope on the hillsides and coyotes may drift along the edges of the coulees. On some of the ridges are "sheepherder monuments" built by unknown men in unknown years.

The sage hen makes short migrations, seemingly to go from one sea of sage to another just like it, the journey performed just the same and at a certain time each year, often at great height. Serious sage grouse hunters may have a record of such movements, which may involve a dozen birds or a thousand.

Although sage grouse seem barely able to become airborne, they fly at good speed once off the ground. Since they are most often shot from the rear and are such heavy birds, heavy loads are needed, shot no smaller than number six, and the light, fast bird gun of woodcock and quail coverts is generally out of place. The serious sage grouse hunter (there aren't many) becomes an expert at gauging the age of multi-colored droppings. His dog may be a stylish pointer or any sort of flusher who will stay within comfortable range. Even binoculars can be a help at sighting moving shadows between sage bushes on distant hills. The sage grouse, who can travel very fast on the ground, has his own tactics. Begin following a flock, and after a long hike a shooter may find that nearly all of the bunch has slipped away in singles and pairs.

The gray partridge, also called Hungarian partridge or simply "Hun," became one of America's top game birds almost by infiltration, making a home, mainly in the West, after repeated introductions had failed early in the 20th century. Although it came from Europe, the term "Hun" is resented by some of its admirers. It lives in pastures with scattered brush and particularly in grain fields — but not necessarily in parts of the country chosen by game managers.

This is a covey bird that flies fast and often maintains a pattern, returning to its original site after several flushes over big country. Pointing dogs work it well but must be cautious of too close an approach. Covey flushes are often confusing, as the bunch may mill wildly before leaving together. There are feeding patterns studied by serious hunters, especially when the birds maintain a schedule of entering stubble fields in the evening.

Light game guns work well with "Huns" and number 7 1/2 shot has been the most popular choice for a bird somewhat larger than quail. As yet, the bird is short on tradition, and many a farmer or rancher who was raised with the sleek immigrant simply calls him a quail. Even today, there are highway tourists who own bird dogs back home and who stop in Western sporting goods shops to learn the name of "those big quail that crossed the highway."

Trained on Pheasants

R ing-necked pheasants in North America today belong to a mixture of races, but all are descended from Asian ancestors. They are members of a species that includes more than thirty subspecies native to the plains of Asia and Asia Minor. The earliest recorded attempt to establish pheasants in the United States was 1773 in New York. Soon after, several subsequent attempts were made but all failed. The first significantly successful stocking in the United States occurred in the Willamette Valley of Oregon in 1881. The birds multiplied so rapidly that within eleven years the first hunting season opened. Thousand of pheasants were shot the first day, and the hunting season lasted more than two months. News of the successful stocking venture in the Far West stimulated individuals, hunting groups, and game departments to get involved in the establishment of the ringneck across North America.

Most of the pheasant range lies in the northern half of United States, below the northern forest. Pheasant populations reached their zenith throughout the country in the 1940s. Then, small farms provided more pheasant habitat, because fields were smaller, with more fence rows that provided cover and edges. As farms grew larger, fences and shelterbelts were removed to provide larger fields. This loss of habitat had a great effect on pheasant populations.

The great pheasant decline started in the early 1950s and never has recovered in most places east of the Mississippi. Despite its severity, pheasant losses in the Northeast, the Great Lakes, and the Midwest did not extend westward.

One of the success stories for the upland

game bird hunter of this decade is reestablished pheasant habitat in many places in the nation, thanks to programs such as the federal Conservation Reserve Program and conservation groups such as Pheasants Forever. When it comes to pheasants today, the largest single block of wild birds is in the breadbasket of the nation, the northern Great Plains states.

Today, more people hunt ring-necked pheasants than any other upland game bird in America. Be it in the wild or on a hunting preserve, to most there's nothing more exciting or unpredictable than the flush of a cackling rooster. The different ways of hunting pheasants are possibly as numerous as pheasant hunters. It's an excellent sport for a battalion of men or one person, young or old. No matter how you choose to hunt, make sure you take away the birds greatest asset — running like a track star. Getting pheasants to fly is the key to successful pheasant hunting, and that requires planning.

The most widely used dog, and perhaps the best, is the Labrador retriever for hunting the ringneck in heavy cover and for finding and retrieving a wounded bird. But any bird dog is better than no dog. Although a large target, once in the air the bird can quickly put distance between it and the gun, and killing the bird is not always easy. A dog takes the worry out of losing this magnificent game bird.

Pheasants need a diversified world of cover, croplands, high grass, cattails and woody riparian waterways, places that trains travel through. With crops harvested and combines gone it's time to go afield hunting the ringneck pheasant.

High Plains Grouse

Members of the Lewis and Clark expedition have been credited with being the first white men to discover the sage grouse. They named the bird "cock of the plains." At the turn of 20th century, the settlers of the West were well acquainted with the sage grouse. It was abundant, and it was not unusual for pioneers to see a flock of hundreds of birds around watering places. The sage grouse is the largest North American grouse (a big male can weigh more than six pounds). I think of them as a Western trophy bird.

Historically, sage grouse inhabited all of the shrub grass prairies of the western United States and Canada. But the years since have not been good for sage grouse. Sagebrush grassland is disappearing at an alarming rate. Thousands of unbroken acres of shrub grasslands are now interspersed with agriculture, to the detriment of the bird's population.

The sage grouse is locked into a single-plant ecosystem. Unlike most other upland game birds, sage grouse depend totally on a single type of plant community. Without sagebrush, sage grouse cannot survive. Sage grouse are still relatively secure in nine states. Although they once faced a dim future, prospects for the sage grouse are now brighter. State and federal wildlife agencies are working hard to restore many square miles of sage grouse country suitable for the birds.

Pursuing them is well worth the effort, and it takes you into country not shared by many. The country, like the bird, is big, wide, and handsome. The sight of twenty or thirty large black and white prairie bombers catapulting into the sky all at once, cutting, passing, and feathering the wind gets your attention. Just seeing the "cock of the plains" airborne is a memorable experience, whether you kill one or not. I have always enjoyed hunting these big, noble birds. Maybe it's because of the habitat in which they live, or maybe it's the wildness of the bird itself — I'm not sure. But I do know it has nothing to with killing this beautiful species. One or two big grouse per season is enough. Prairie bombers are special, and with pointing dogs it's a pleasure. Charley Waterman said it best, "When sage chickens flush, there are shadows on the prairie."

When hunting sage grouse, think in terms of walking long distances. The grouse is big like the country. There's a lot more sagebrush than sage grouse and the habitat hides its secrets well. Hopefully, you'll find a bird or two and also a little water so the dogs can cool down.

SHARP-TAILED GROUSE

Prairie Feathers

Say "steppe grouse," and most hunters won't recognize it. But mention sharp-tailed grouse to the same hunters and they would immediately know it as a bird of the open prairies, even though sharptails are found in greater number in grasslands, savannas, and sagebrush plains (steppes). Their habitat also includes natural grasslands with low sage, open woodland, extensive brushy openings in logged forests of the Great Lakes, and the extensive "muskegs" of the boreal forest region.

Today, the sharptail is the most abundant grouse on the steppes and one of the important native game birds hunted throughout its range. There are six subspecies that occupy suitable habitat over a huge area of North America. Their range covers more than twelve states, part of the Yukon and the Northwest Territory, and six Canadian Provinces.

In the early days, much of the northern Midwest had a beautiful combination of prairie woodlands and open meadows, and these were the prevailing places to hunt the sharp-tailed grouse. When settled, much of the land was cleared and the prairie chicken moved in and occupied the same general areas as the sharptail. As time passed, much of the cleared land reverted back to its original habitat and the sharp-tailed grouse returned in abundance, replacing the prairie chicken. Today, sharptails outnumber prairie chickens in all their overlapping range.

The sharptail eats a wider variety of food than any other upland game bird, even the buds of tall trees in winter, ensuring its survival. Few other game birds have this capacity to survive. The sharptail has done what the passenger pigeon and the prairie chicken could not. Each subspecies adapted to a different type of habitat when man

Grasslands, Foothills, and Farmlands

changed the landscape. It flourished before and after the plow, in the forest and after it was cleared.

Sharptails are not covey birds, though they do flock into loose groups. Few prairie game birds can thrill the hunter more than a large flock of grouse busting for cover. It takes a good pointer, whatever the breed, to learn to hunt sharptails, and it may well be one of the hardest game birds for a dog to adjust to. Sharptails give inexperienced dogs fits. Every species of game bird has to be approached differently with pointing dogs, and adult sharptails are a lot different than the young birds that Southern boys come north to train their "pointen dogs" on.

High up the springlet, I encountered the old homestead. Abandoned buildings and windbreaks of chokecherries, wild roses, and scattered lilacs planted years past by the woman of the house are good sharptail hangouts. You should be there when the chokecherries ripen.

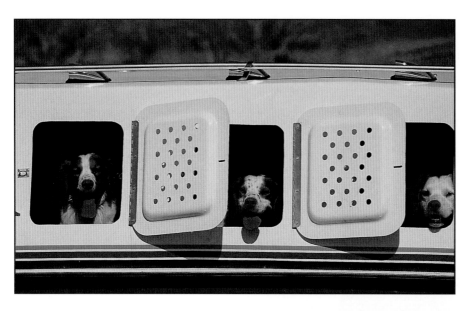

GRAY PARTRIDGE

Birds of Open Spaces

I f you are hunting in the shortgrass prairie, listen to the prairie, for it will tell you where to find the gray partridge. If you are hunting country turned by the plow, listen to the uncut edges.

Gray partridge originated in the vast steppes of Central Europe long before the Great Plains were used for agriculture. As the nation's grasslands became cultivated, the gray partridge adapted to the new environment and flourished as long as the habitat was not abruptly changed. Today, the bird thrives in both the open prairies and the grain belts of North America.

The first introductions of gray partridge in North America were before 1900. Many of the birds were imported from Hungary; hence the name Hungarian partridge or Hun. Most plantings of the bird east of the Mississippi were not successful. A little later

Hungarian partridge were liberated in Washington and Oregon with limited success. The successful introductions occurred in Alberta and Saskatchewan, and these plantings spread southward to Washington, Idaho, Montana, and North Dakota. Today, the gray partridge continues to spread throughout the prairie provinces of Canada and the northern plains states west of the Great Lakes.

I have hunted every upland game bird in North America, and after pursuing the gray partridge for more than forty years it is still my favorite. Why? To me it is the quail of the Northern Plains. It's a covey bird that sometimes lies as tight as a covey of bobwhite, and other times the birds run and flush as wild as a covey of Gambel's quail.

Like the ruffed grouse and woodcock, the Hun is a bird made for pointing dogs. But the gray partridge dog has to be different than the dog of the forest. For the most part, the Hun dog has to be fast and far-ranging. For me, when hunting Hungarian partridge, a brace of dogs or more is better. Dogs need exceptional noses to pick up the birds' scent at great distances. Unlike many other game birds, gray partridge will flush when approached too closely, so a dog must learn the ways of a Hun when pointing. If a dog has these essential qualities, it will be able to lock up one covey of Huns after another.

Gray partridge coveys are widely scattered in big, open country and at times can be difficult to locate. But once found and flushed, the covey is the most explosive and fastest upland game bird on the wing. On the first flush, the covey usually stays in tight formation, flying a short distance. Most members of the covey land in the same vicinity and can be located again. After several flushes, the birds scatter into singles and doubles, which hold tight, much like single bobwhites.

To me, hunting Huns, "the big quail of the Northern Plains" is much like hunting the king of the game birds, the bobwhite.

We'll hike to where the gray partridge may be feeding along the slopes of rolling hills, along the edges of old wooden fence rows or the sage brush draws that run into grain fields. Finding gray partridge requires lots of walking and big running dogs. They're birds of sweeping grain fields and open prairies that run for miles.

Grassland Grouse

o other game bird lent a greater charm to the prairies than the true prairie chicken. The bird was there long before the gray partridge or pheasant. No sound evoked more feeling than the early morning booming of a prairie chicken from a high hill close to a homestead or a distant knoll above a ranch house. No game bird has thrilled the young hunter more than a prairie chicken flushing from under a dog's nose, gun half ready, and the rest of the flock getting up in all directions. Of all the grouse in the early 1900s, the prairie chicken undoubtedly furnished the most satisfaction to the average sportsmen. It was the peoples' bird — the ranch hand, the farmer who toiled in the field, and the townfolk. The bird had no rival; it came and went with the sodbusters.

The prairie chicken once inhabited all the prairies of the United States east of the Rockies and well into many prairie provinces of Canada. Today, this species occupies only a small faction of its original range. During the first half of the century, almost all of the virgin prairie sod was torn by the plow. The tall, graceful grasses gave way to grain fields and left the black soil exposed for months. This game bird thrived with the first wave of settlers, held its own when the population doubled, then faded when civilization finally tamed most of the prairie.

Although the prairie chicken adapted to the changing conditions and followed the plow, as did the bobwhite quail, it could not endure the destruction of most of its range. So great was the loss of prairie habitat that only a few states still have the large, open areas necessary for the birds' survival. Today, it is these mixed prairie grasslands properly managed that furnish the cover that is vital to the prairie chicken's nesting, roosting, and booming grounds.

By September, young birds are as big as the adults. The bird is a strong flyer and shooting is challenging. The best dog for chicken hunting is any dog that likes to hunt, be it a pointer, setter, flusher, or retriever. To many Westerners, the prairie chicken is still the bird of the people, and people have many breeds of dogs.

In fall, prairie grasslands are golden and waving in the wind. The distance to the horizon will stretch one's eye. This year, the grass is tall and the chickens are here. Make sure to take plenty of supplies — towns are few and far between.

97

Grasslands, Foothills, and Farmlands

Part Three

Desert and Tundra

Desert and Tundra

Introduction

by Charley F. Waterman

The desert can be hot, even during quail season, and midday may find the desert quail in seclusion, probably sought by a golden eagle, a graceful raptor riding his chosen thermal against a very blue sky. The Gambel's quail, somehow watchful from secluded spots guarded by plants that scratch and stab, is a runner like the scaled quail and the valley quail.

There are locales where the Gambel bird seldom flies, and otherwise sportsmanlike shotgunners may resort to shooting them on the ground, quick shots at darting shadows glimpsed through cactus forests. And there are times when the gunner's percentage may be lower than he would expect with other birds that fly as game birds are supposed to. The Gambel's quail and the valley quail are almost duplicates, the latter

especially noted for enormous coveys that may be here today and gone tomorrow. Time was when commercial hunters gathered valley quail by the thousands in water hole ambushes, and the Gambel's probably faced the same pressure in other locales. Both are victims of road hunting but will perform for pointing dogs if the hunters are patient.

The scaled quail, also called blue quail or cottontop, tends to fly as a last resort and is dreaded by some pointing dog perfectionists. Furtive shadows moving in almost impenetrable cactus can cause nervous breakdowns for dogs trained in classic ways. The cottontop not only leads as a sprinter, it has confusing flight patterns and tends to fly higher than the other desert quail when flushed. Many athletic hunters chase blues without dogs, and coveys are often first

sighted from vehicles. There is low comedy in a gunner trying to make an instantaneous escape from a pickup truck with a long-barreled pump gun. There is disagreement as to what should be yelled to make the birds fly when a sprinter is in full pursuit.

Equipment for the desert quails (and the variety of very similar quails of the less arid West) is a little difficult to select, for there is such a wide variety of terrain and vegetation. The panting pursuer of cottontops is likely to use a long-range gun when they finally fly, but some hunters of valley quail may find themselves peering into the depths of a bush where a single has disappeared and refuses to leave. One hunter, who had scattered a huge covey over a western hillside, said he needed two tools — a duck gun and a butterfly net. So it is hard to classify a bird that dawdles about backyards but sizzles around a hillside.

"We had a pretty good day," said the tourist gunner, "but I'm not sure just what kind of quail we got."

In the true desert country, visiting hunters need to know about poisonous snakes and a number of smaller creatures that bite and sting. Such advance knowledge makes the country look a lot less forbidding. Dog users need pliers for cactus, and in some localities dog boots are a help.

Many desert experts have little hope of flushing a tight covey at reasonable range and plan instead to scatter the birds. Then they hunt the singles and pairs they may have marked down, or at least watched for some distance. Such methods are hard to teach to a pointing dog, but some learn the game quickly.

The tundra, despite its great concentration of plant and animal life, is often considered something of a wasteland, and its ptarmigan are mystery birds to most sportsmen. With all the stories of starving miners who have killed them with sticks, many regard them as "fool hens," a name that has been applied to almost all upland birds at one time or another as a matter of location and circumstance. Then, from time to time a serious bird hunter sets forth to examine the ptarmigan as a sporting proposition, usually finding it is too easy or too difficult.

Although they are hunted much the same and look much alike, there are three different birds: the willow ptarmigan of creek bottoms; the rock ptarmigan of the high slopes; and the white-tailed ptarmigan of the mountain peaks — except in winter, when the three types may be found almost together.

Any cold-weather ptarmigan hunt can be hard work, but even in the warmest of Alaska weather the birds may be hard to collect. When found at high altitudes in screaming winds, the birds may remain unseen until they dive almost straight down from a ledge where they have fitted into the stony landscape.

On tundra ridges they may regard a hunter with idle curiosity, or even move closer to inspect a pointing dog. But the ability of an early fall ptarmigan in blotchy plumage to blend into a pattern of blotchy stones seems almost supernatural.

The movements of ptarmigan flocks can be forecast only through careful study, and even the expert can make bad guesses. For that matter, even a professional biologist may have trouble differentiating sample skins of the three recognized kinds of ptarmigan.

Ptarmigan hunting can be windy and wet, if not cold, and some of the undulating tundra can be a little like walking on a stack of feather beds. From time to time it has been discovered that dogs point ptarmigan well, but there are many situations where a pointer is unnecessary and the flushing breeds work well if kept within range. Serious hunting will probably be most successful with guns and loads that can handle a husky bird at forty yards.

Desert Points

The Gambel's quail, also called the desert quail of the Southwest, is a replica of its northern cousin, the valley quail. The size and color is quite similar except for the under parts.

The Gambel's habits are almost identical to the valley quail's, but its habitat is considerably different. He lives in a harsh but beautiful country. Unlike his neighbor, the scaled quail, which occupies some of the same range but lives in chaparral and grasslands habitat, the Gambel's quail prefers a more rugged environment. Generally speaking, the Gambel's quail is a bird of the brushy desert and thorny forest, full of mesquite, cholla, yucca, cactus, and other plants unfriendly to those who trespass. The Gambel's quail is native to the southwestern United States and northwestern Mexico. It has been established after introduction in several other locations, too. The Gambel's

quail is the most important game in the Southwest. Its popularity as a sporting bird in the desert country is equal to the bobwhite's popularity in the Midwest.

The Gambel's quail is a fast little target and can give any upland bird hunter some real shooting thrills. Besides fine wingshooting, you may find yourself gripped by a real passion for the breathtaking desert. In the morning, the low light casts long, graceful shadows across the cacti landscape. At midday the desert has a singular loneliness lurking in its beauty. Evening, with its golden light, softens the harshness of the sun and transforms the desert in to a world of loveliness.

Many hunters, however, hesitate to use dogs in such tough country because of the abundance of cacti. But I don't. If the condition warrants, I use dog boots. I believe the dogs like the boots and think they are something special. The Gambel's

quail can be hunted without dogs, but after the covey is scattered, the birds sit tightly, and sometimes are almost impossible to flush without a dog.

As a rule, when a large flock of desert quail is found, the birds must be scattered by man or dog. After the birds are scattered, experienced hunters know they're in for some great shooting. For many hunters there is nothing finer than working a pointing dog on a large, broken covey of tight-holding Gambel's for an half hour or so. This is the time when a good bird dog earns its biscuit. This is also when the desert quail behaves much like its distant cousin, the bobwhite, and may flush unexpectedly and fly up your shirt sleeve.

Gambel's quail like rugged country. It's a bird of the thorny forest full of mesquite and other plants unfriendly to those who trespass. The desert may seem hostile to a hunting dog, but most adapt. Make sure to give your dog lots of water and check his pads often.

SCALED QUAIL

Cottontops over Brittanys

It was near Felt, Oklahoma, where I first saw the scaled quail. The gas station attendant asked if I was looking for cottontops. The grocer told me to hunt the Rita Blanca Wildlife Management Area if I wanted blue quail. Scaled, blue, or cottontop quail are one in the same. The scaled quail's native range includes the arid sections of the southwestern United States and the northern areas of Mexico. It's a familiar game bird of the grassy desert uplands. Unlike the Gambel's quail, the scaled quail prefers sparse vegetation. Because of the open cover, this quail is a notorious runner and would rather not fly to escape its enemies.

Scaled quail congregate in large coveys numbering forty to fifty or more. Large groups usually have to be broken up to have close shooting. Dogs certainly help to scatter the birds. Once the covey is scattered, singles and small group of birds hold extremely tightly.

The scaled quail is quick to take advantage of feed or water around ranches and farmsteads, since the necessities of life are never overabundant in the desert.

Late one afternoon several summers after my first encounter with scaled quail, I was driving through the same area of Oklahoma. The temperature was well over one hundred degrees, and, like most desert creatures, the scaled quail is rarely out in the bright, hot sun. I turned off the main road, onto a dirt lane that wandered through a brushy arroyo full of juniper, mesquite, and cactus, and stopped by a old farmstead. A windmill was singing a see-saw tune when I stepped out of the pickup to water my dogs. A nearby puddle, the overflow from a stock tank, was only an inch deep, but the dogs wallowed in it to take advantage of the coolness of the water. Life surrounding the abandoned farm-stead seemed nonexistent. Nothing moved except the wind pushing against the blades of the windmill. No sound was heard except the grinding of the windmill's gears and the dogs splashing what little water there was. I walked toward a weathered barn. The sky had darkened. The windmill stopped briefly while the blade housing spun one hundred eighty degrees. Then the blades became a blur from the force of the west wind. Lightning flashed while I was putting the dogs up, and as I sat in the driver's seat a torrential rain blocked my view though the windshield. The puddle became a small lake, then the deluge stopped as quickly as it started, but the sky did not clear. I rolled down the window and was about to pull out when suddenly, several flocks of quail materialized and songbirds emerged from nowhere. I could smell the fragrant wet sand, and the sounds of nature filled my ears.

Hunting scaled quail is not like hunting Mearns', Gambel's, or bobwhite. For one thing, the scaled quail's cruising range is larger. Scaled quail are like a desert breeze — one day they're all around you, the next day they're gone.

To the Point

Let us imagine the opening day of the quail season in one of the far Western states — bright, warm weather and most of the vegetation still green. Weeds stand tall from the spring rains along the creek. Around the fields, fences are lined with brush displaying red and golden berries. The steep, rocky hillsides are carpeted by cheatgrass, and silver-blue sage fills the autumn air with aromatic splendor.

The sun has been up for several hours as two men work the cover with a pair of pointing dogs. There is no need to hurry; if quail are there, the dogs will find them. The murmur of running water is broken by the sound of the dogs' beepers. The dogs have something pointed. There is no reason to quicken the pace as both hunters move toward the dogs. Suddenly there's a roar of wings made by the flush of quail and loud reports from the guns. Silence settles

over the riparian forest, broken only by dogs crashing though the brush for the retrieves as the large covey of quail scatters across the creek and fans out on the steep sage hillside.

Valley quail are fast flyers. But they generally fly only a short distance and can be found again. Critics of the bird may tell you that they cannot be worked with pointing dogs, but that is a myth. Some pointing dogs may have difficulty with a covey of valley quail, but singles and doubles will lie as well as their cousins, the bobwhite quail. Without a dog, single birds become very difficult to flush. So a good dog is essential for finding a scattered covey and retrieving cripples.

The valley quail, also called the California quail, is a native of California and Nevada. Live trapping and transplanting the bird to similar habitat extended its original range to include all of the Pacific coastal states, western New Mexico, Idaho, Nevada, and Utah. The birds preferred habitat is brush, grassland, and mixed farming, such as fallow fields, hedgerows, and streamside hardwood thickets

The habits of the quail vary with the weather and season. On warm days, singles hold tightly and rarely run. If the day is wet or rainy, valley quail have a tendency to flush wild or run after landing. All species of North American quail are gregarious, but the valley quail tops the list when it comes to large flocks. As winter approaches and food and cover dwindles, coveys join together, forming large groups of as many as three hundred birds. These large flocks have a better chance of winter survival, and late in the season the birds are hard to approach. But once a large flock is broken up, the singles and doubles lie well for dogs.

Valley quail are gregarious, gathering in large flocks in the fall, sometimes numbering in the hundreds. Although the birds have the reputation for being runners, once broken up they'll hold as tight as bobwhites. When a large flock is scattered shooting can be fast and furious.

Ptarmigan on the Ptundra

There are three species of ptarmigan: the willow ptarmigan, the rock ptarmigan, and the white-tailed ptarmigan. All three are found in cold, windswept tundra and alpine regions of the Northern Hemisphere. Each kind of ptarmigan lives in a slightly different environment than the others. The willow and rock ptarmigan are circumpolar, whereas the white-tailed ptarmigan only lives in the high western mountains of North America. The white-tailed ptarmigan lives in higher elevations — land of rugged scree and snow field. Rock ptarmigan occupy the middle slopes and low, rocky ridges. The willow ptarmigan chooses the marshy tundra and shrub country close to the timberline.

Ptarmigan are nomadic, gathering in large groups and traveling great distances in search of food in the fall. Flocks of birds during the winter months can number in the thousands. Ptarmigan are quite sociable in winter and usually feed and roost close together.

The willow ptarmigan is found nearly everywhere in the treeless country of Alaska, Canada, Greenland, Iceland, Scotland, Scandinavia, Russia, and northern Eurasia.

The most famous upland game bird of the British Isles is the red grouse. "The Glorious Twelfth of August" is the opening of the grouse season, and at one time this day was almost a national holiday. Britons gather from all parts of the globe to shoot the moors for red grouse on the mother land. But the red grouse is the same fine game bird as our willow ptarmigan. In North America they are still numerous, and in Alaska the season starts on the "Glorious Tenth of August."

The average American hunter, however, knows little about the willow ptarmigan, even though its range exceeds that of most other game birds. I have hunted them in Alaska at different times during the nine-month hunting season and have found them always challenging. The ptarmigan is a unique bird to hunt and has several characteristics that I believe puts it in a class by itself. It is a bird of the extreme Far North and the only game bird you can collect in three different color phases during the course of a hunting season.

Early autumn may be the best time to hunt willow ptarmigan, because this is the time the birds are in small flocks. Although I prefer to hunt with a pointing dog, ptarmigan are easy to approach early in the season, making a dog unnecessary. Willow ptarmigan lie tight for a pointing dog and are as rapid a flyer as any grouse. Once you find the birds, shooting can be fast, with birds flushing in all directions. Later in the season the small flocks gather together, disperse, and form again into larger groups that are sometimes hard to approach.

American Wingshooting

In early fall, when the high shrubs still have green leaves and the muskeg is full of blueberries, take your hunting dog for an airplane ride over the tundra. Find a place to land, get out, look around, and go hunting. You'll probably be surrounded by ptarmigan and I'm sure your dog will enjoy it.

Winter hunting for willow ptarmigan is different, but it is still the same fine grouse even though the bird's color has changed. Bundle up, put on the snowshoes, and if the snow is not too deep take along your bird dog.

Part Four

Mountains and Conifers

Mountains and Conifers

Introduction

by Charley F. Waterman

It has created a following of hunters with battered shotguns, scuffed boots, and a love of crumbling mountains and slopes of cheatgrass. Having gained a high foothold in the West in the early 1950s, it may be the chukar partridge is the most distinctive of all American upland game.

Although their equipment usually bears similar scars, chukar gunners go about the sport in several ways. Perhaps the most dramatic is the sure-footed climber with the open-bored shotgun and no dog, who slips silently about the high rimrocks, whether he has heard cackling or not, and may hear the nearby scuffle of chukar feet. The flush is likely to be at close range and part of his challenge is to find a shooting position in split seconds. He may have located the birds hours before if the wind is right, but despite a common belief, chukars do not always cackle. Still, the expert knows the right terrain and reads the sign accurately.

Chukar hunters with different backgrounds may have little in common. The game preserve chukar is often criticized as being too easy a target, but it depends upon how the bird was raised. One that will ride happily in a covered basket bears little resemblance to the high-altitude runner and diver who plunges below a gun barrel and is finally seen again by a frustrated shooter as only a glint of wings far out over a rocky abyss. Not only is the individual bird's immediate ancestry important, so is the location of its kin. Chukar populations move in unexplained ways, with this year's concentration found where the population was "down" last year. Chukar counting in their favorite

mountains is a frustrating task.

There are chukar experts who drive high backcountry trails, especially in dry weather, and scrutinize rocky creeks where birds come for water. Then, when birds are located, they make elaborate stalks. There are less ethical hunters who hope to catch a covey in the road and will shoot after a hurried dismount — or even from a truck. And, of course, there are those who use flushing or pointing dogs, believing that dog work is an essential part of the game.

The spruce grouse and blue grouse are quite similar in attitudes toward hunters and fit the classification of fool hen in undisturbed and timbered surrounding. After being hunted, they can be difficult enough, but many of them are shot from trees by big game hunters to spice up a camp diet. The blue is found at low altitude early in the season, migrating to the windswept high ridges as the weather chills. As the season opens, they can often be found on open hillsides, prime targets for pointing or flushing dogs. Later, the hunting will require some climbing, and hunters argue the dog question. The spruce grouse will live at about the same altitude year-round.

The Western ruffed grouse has never had much hunting pressure, and a New England grouse gunner with a specialized dog will often insist that the Westerner is a completely different bird. In the Rockies, a ruff is likely to sit fully exposed on a conifer branch and observe hunters with interest. But the traveling New Englander or Midwesterner is wrong. It's the same bird, and after hearing a few shots it resorts to some of the tactics of its better educated relatives.

There are times when the usually canny ruff can be too easy, even when pointed on the ground in brushy surroundings. There are some Canadian spots where the "willow grouse" (Canadian designation) will stand in a narrow path and bristle at a befuddled interloper with a quick little shotgun. Worst of all is the situation in which early season grouse, still in family coveys, can be caught by pointers unable to withstand the sight of a cluster of birds scurrying about in indecision.

But with a little experience, the Western ruffed grouse becomes deceptive and can leave in thunder. It's really the same bird.

CHUKAR PARTRIDGE

Rugged Walk for Rock Partridge

Hunting chukar takes you into rocky country — places wild horses roam. The story of establishing the chukar in America is as amazing as the bird is unusual. Nearly every state and several provinces of Canada tried to introduced chukars into the wild and all early efforts failed. Later, it was realized that the Rocky Mountain region had areas similar to the bird's native origin, so new attempts were made, but with limited success. Several years later, in 1935, chukars were introduce in country that closely resembled its native Asian ranges. The rocky, arid, open uplands of Nevada were ideal, and within a decade the first hunting season for chukars opened in the United States. The success of the chukar was so outstanding in Nevada that other states with similar habitat released wild birds

and the chukar partridge spread like wildfire. Today there are ten western states with huntable populations.

The chukar is a bird that thrives in high, arid country full of sagebrush, greasewood, bunch grass, and cheatgrass. Steep canyon walls, talus slopes, rocky outcroppings, cliffs, bluffs, barren windswept ridges, and desert conditions are to the bird's liking. During hot, dry weather the birds will congregate around water to drink and feed on lush greens.

Chukars are a sociable bird and form large flocks in early fall and winter. Chukars have keen eyesight and when approached, even from long distances, will usually run uphill, stopping short of a hilltop so they can watch their pursuer.

Chukar hunting is for the young, or at least the young at heart. It can be the most strenuous and exhausting bird hunting in America. I'm not talking about driving country roads, looking for coveys, I'm talking about hard hiking for this fine, exotic game bird.

Chukars do a lot of calling early in the morning and in late afternoon, and listening for the bird's location can be highly productive. Chukars have the same habits as other game birds. They feed, water, loaf, dust, and rest at certain times throughout the day. Learning these places can save a lot of boot leather.

In chukar country, pointing dogs help. Dogs can save the hunter a lot of walking over the course of a day. When a large covey is located and scattered, hunting becomes a lot easier. Chukars are very vocal when the covey is broken up, and they start calling soon after being separated. After you flush a covey, don't get in a hurry. Stop, wait, and listen for several minutes before going on. Chukars do not fly great distances, but depend on the rugged terrain for their escape. Small groups of birds lie extremely well for a pointing dog, so shooting can be close. Chukars on the wing are fast and the target is not easy. Many shots are at birds screaming down a steep incline.

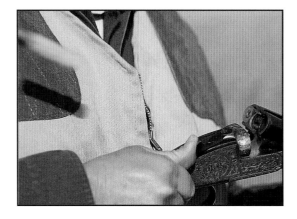

When hunting chukar country, dogs can save you lots of shoe leather over the course of a day. It has been said that chukar always run up and fly down, but don't believe it. It all depends on the bird's best escape route after the flush.

SPRUCE GROUSE

Fool Hen, Fool Men

It has been said by many writers and hunters that the "fool hen" is not a worthwhile or very sporting game bird, but I disagree. The spruce grouse often refuses to fly when approached by a hunter, but a true sportsman will only shoot it on the wing. When the bird does fly, however, it can be missed easily. The bird always seems to put a tree between itself and the gunner. Today, the spruce grouse is still called "fool hen," but it can fool you.

Forest grouse that live in primitive country have no natural fear of man. The bird depends on its wings for escape and feels secure on the ground, out of the reach of any ground predator. Early settlers named the ruffed grouse the fool hen because of the grouse's lack of fear of man. The constant presence of man and hunting pressure over the years educated the Eastern ruffed grouse to the keen quarry it is today. As the settlers moved

west, the name "fool hen" was passed along to other game birds that had no fear of man. Even a few of the prairie game birds shared this name. Woodsmen have known the spruce grouse ever since the first days of human settlement and the name "fool hen," if used at all, should be reserved for the spruce grouse.

Even today, there are still many miles of backwoods and alpine forest that are not visited by the hunter, and these are the places where spruce grouse live. Nearly every good stand of boreal forest in North America has its population of spruce grouse. The year-round range of the spruce grouse is enormous, extending from Alaska to the Northwest Territories to Labrador and southward into New England and westward into the northern Rocky Mountains of the western United states.

It was once commonly believed that the

fool hen was found only in the deepest spruce forest. Such is not the case, in my experience. The coniferous forest in which the birds live is dense and sometimes difficult to penetrate, but I hunt along logging road, mountain trails, cattle trails, and openings around the edges of the forest while the dog works the heavy cover. Along the bordered openings and brushy creeks a dog is especially helpful and can find a bird that a hunter would pass by. When a grouse is flushed from the ground it invariably goes to heavy cover, and if missed by the shot it will usually fly to an evergreen tree. Getting the grouse out of the tree can be a real challenge and a very difficult wing shot. If one is lucky enough to get a shot and put a bird on the ground, a dog is invaluable in finding the grouse in such dense cover.

Spruce grouse are different birds when you find them off the road. In the deep woods, the bird has a habit of bringing your shooting average down. Sometimes you'll find the birds feeding within fifty yards; other times you won't find them at all. They're there and with a good dog you'll find them eventually.

Going up the Mountain

The blue grouse is the second largest of the nine North American grouse. It is more closely related to the sage grouse than to the spruce grouse and may have evolved from prairie grouse. Like the sage grouse, the breeding and nesting range occurs in steppe and grassland habitat. But unlike their prairie cousins, blue grouse live close to the edges and lower open parks of the montane forest. The fall movement, sometimes called the autumn migration, of blue grouse is from the open breeding areas to the denser conifer forest. This is the only upland game bird in North America that moves from a lower elevation to a higher elevation in winter. During this period, virtually all of the birds' winter food is conifer needles.

Hunting blue grouse early in the season is quite different from hunting them later on. At the opening of the season, however, blues usually will not be far from brushy draws and open meadows, close to streams or springs, where they search for berries, greens, grasshoppers, and other insects. When the birds are in the lower country is the easiest time of year to hunt them. But it is not always the most productive time, because there is more food available and the family groups are more scattered. Young birds in remote areas are quite tame and will let a dog approach or point them within wingshooting range. Dogs are extremely useful when hunting blue grouse, as they hold well for pointing dogs. When flushed, blues, like other forest grouse, will often fly toward some type of thick cover and out of sight in a matter of seconds.

Later in the season, the birds will have moved to higher elevations on ridges with mixed open parks and conifers. Hunting blues then becomes more strenuous, because the hunter has to climb steep hills and mountains to find them. Blue grouse concentrate in certain areas at this time of year and one may have to do a lot of hiking to find them. But when you do find them, chances are the birds will be in groups of six to ten and dispersed across a whole ridge top. Often a hunter will see a bird on the ground and watch it fly to nearby tree. Getting the bird to fly from a tall pine or spruce tree and then shooting the grouse as it swoops down is difficult. Also, when flushed from the ground the bird will invariably fly downhill, gaining speed and going out of sight.

Sometimes the best blue grouse hunting is not along an old logging road, but off the road in heavy cover. Walk the ridges high above the valley floor. Take a rest often. The scenery is will worth the walk and you may even bag a big blue grouse or two.

RANGE MAPS

Present Distribution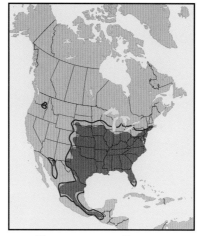
Historical Range ————
Winter Range ————

Note: There are many gaps within present ranges due to loss of habitat and human activity

KEY

BOBWHITE QUAIL

RUFFED GROUSE

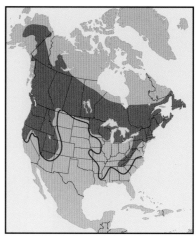

WOODCOCK

MEARN'S QUAIL

MOURNING DOVE

PHEASANT

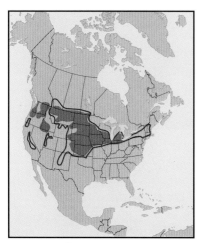

SAGE GROUSE

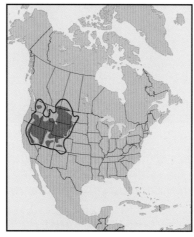

SHARP-TAILED GROUSE

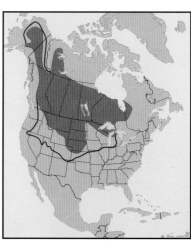

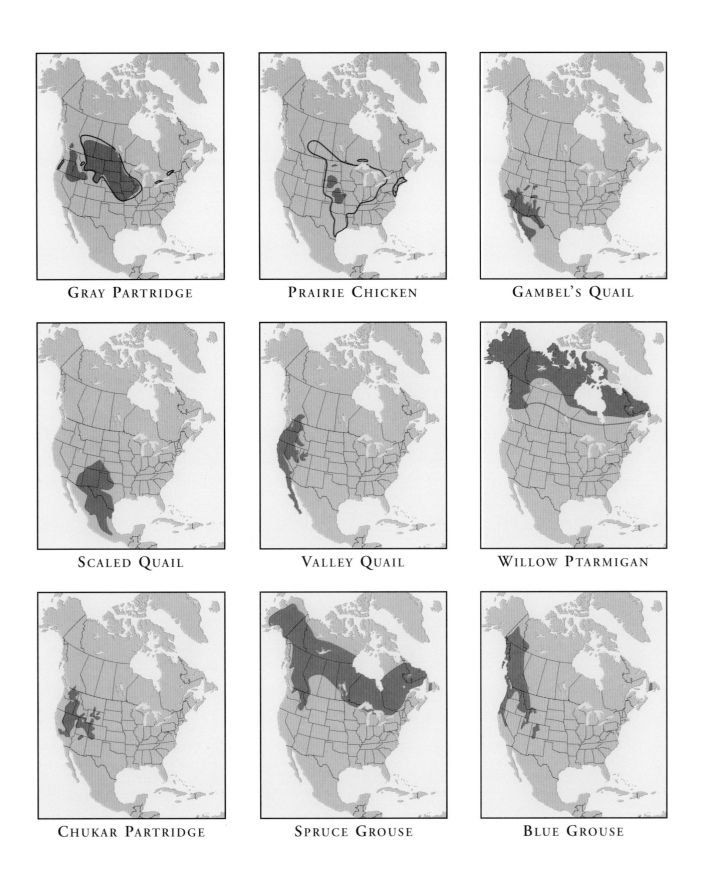

GRAY PARTRIDGE

PRAIRIE CHICKEN

GAMBEL'S QUAIL

SCALED QUAIL

VALLEY QUAIL

WILLOW PTARMIGAN

CHUKAR PARTRIDGE

SPRUCE GROUSE

BLUE GROUSE